ELIE WIESEL

JEAN SILVERMAN
AND LINDA BAYER

Published in 2016 by The Rosen Publishing Group, Inc.
29 East 21st Street, New York, NY 10010

Library of Congress Cataloging-in-Publication Data

Silverman, Jean, 1976- author.
Elie Wiesel / Jean Silverman and Linda Bayer. -- First edition.
    pages cm -- (The Holocaust)
Includes bibliographical references and index.
ISBN 978-1-4994-6250-0 (library bound)
1. Wiesel, Elie, 1928---Juvenile literature. I. Title.
PQ2683.I32Z875 2015
940.53'18092--dc23

                                                                2015032167

Manufactured in China

CONTENTS

INTRODUCTION

During World War II (1939–1945), Nazi Germany devised what it called "the Final Solution." This was a government-sanctioned plan for the systematic rounding up, imprisonment, torture, and extermination of the Jewish race. The plan was the brainchild of Adolf Hitler, a madman dictator who believed Jews were tainting German culture. His goal was a "pure" Aryan race.

The Holocaust is considered the most horrifying and shameful episode in modern history. It resulted in the slaughter of six million Jewish men, women, and children. Families were torn apart. Homes were abandoned and fortunes lost. Neighbor turned against neighbor. Good people were dehumanized and forced to endure unspeakable conditions.

Elie Wiesel experienced the horrors of the Holocaust. He made sure that his survival had a purpose. To honor those lost, including several family members, Wiesel has worked tirelessly to make sure we never forget the atrocities committed by Adolf Hitler and his anti-Semitic Nazi regime.

Those who managed to survive this nightmare, fortunate though they were to be alive, had a lot to overcome. When they went to bed at night, they remembered sharing overcrowded bunks and never feeling fully rested. When they closed their eyes, they saw people being beaten to death by sadistic guards. They saw innocent babies being burned in ditches and lines of people being marched to gas chambers. How could anyone who had witnessed those horrors ever find peace again?

As a teenager in the Romanian countryside before the war, Elie Wiesel watched as Jews were increasingly marginalized in Germany and through-out Europe. He saw the wave of anti-Semitism find his village, and before he knew it, he and his family were boarding cattle cars bound for the Auschwitz concentration camp. There, he and his father were separated from his mother and sisters. What fol-lowed was a year of unimaginable terror until Allied troops finally liberated the camps.

Although he was safe, he was hardly free. He had lost his family, his homeland, his childhood. And he had seen the worst of humanity. How could he possibly live a normal life?

After years of nightmares, soul searching, and a self-imposed vow of silence about the Holocaust, Wiesel finally found the words to write about his experience. This led to teaching positions, in which he educated students about the Holocaust, genocide, and human rights. Eventually, he entered the world stage, meeting with world leaders and other public officials to ensure the Holocaust would never be forgotten, that the one positive thing to result from that chapter of history is that it would never happen again.

The truth is, genocide and violations of human rights have continued to occur around the world. That is what makes Wiesel's life's work so vital. His tireless efforts to "never forget" have earned him countless awards, including the Nobel Peace Prize and the Presidential Medal of Freedom, and his continued push to fight on behalf of the powerless is his greatest legacy.

CHAPTER ONE

EARLY LIFE

Elie Wiesel was born in 1928 in Sighet, Romania. His parents, Shlomo and Sarah, had married for love. This was an unusual practice during a time when marriages arranged by parents or matchmakers were more common. As the story goes, Shlomo Wiesel spotted Sarah riding in a carriage and was awestruck by her beauty. The young couple married a year later and had two daughters, Hilda and Bea, before Sarah gave birth to Elie, their only son. Elie was followed by sister Tsiporah, the baby of the family.

Elie was named after his grandfather, Eliezer, who had been killed during World War I while working as a stretcher-bearer not far from the village where the Wiesels lived. Shlomo Wiesel, a shopkeeper and a leader in his community, was widely respected for his wisdom and common sense. Sarah Wiesel was the daughter of a respected rabbi. Young Elie learned reason and humanitarianism from his father and faith from his mother.

A LOVE OF FAMILY AND FAITH

Elie was a serious, shy, sickly child who preferred books to sports. Chess was the one game he enjoyed. Intimidated by classmates at an early age, Elie often feigned illness so he could stay home with the mother he adored.

An insecure youngster, Elie tried to bribe his classmates with fruit, buttered bread, and other snacks in hopes of winning their affection. Later, he offered presents and even money taken from the till at his father's grocery store. Even still, the children scorned Elie, who remained somewhat apart.

BAR MITZVAH

Elie Wiesel has said that he became increasingly more religious in the years following his bar mitzvah. The bar mitzvah is a religious rite of passage marking a Jewish boy's entry into manhood at age thirteen. This means the boy is responsible for fulfilling all the commandments.

The youngster's maturation is celebrated in the synagogue by his standing before the congregation, chanting aloud in Hebrew and saying blessings over the Torah scrolls containing the Five Books of Moses.

The adulthood of girls is marked with a ceremony called the Bat Mitzvah.

On Friday nights and Saturdays, however, Elie loved being at home with his family, singing songs around the festive table. Six days a week, Shlomo Wiesel worked at the small grocery store he owned. Shabbat was the one time during the week when Elie spent time with his father, who often invited dinner guests—especially beggars and other poor souls unable to afford food—to celebrate the Sabbath.

On the seventh day, according to the Bible, God rested from all his work creating the earth. Observant Jews follow Sabbath laws that prohibit all forms of work on this day. Instead, eating, praying in synagogue, studying religious texts, and relaxing are prescribed activities. As Elie grew older, he continued to enjoy the Sabbath and practice all its rituals. At eight years of age, Elie accompanied his mother—as he did every year—to seek a blessing of health and well-being from Rabbi Israel of Wizhnitz, who had come to visit Sighet. After asking Elie

to sit on his lap and review the lessons the boy was learning in *heder* (religious school), the rabbi asked Elie to leave the room while he imparted a special message to the boy's mother. Sarah Wiesel began

Elie Wiesel grew up in Sighet, a village in Romania that was reassigned to Hungary in 1940 as a result of the Second Vienna Award. The Jewish community in Sighet was strong, and Elie Wiesel's family was very active within it. This photograph shows members of Sighet's Jewish community in front of their synagogue in the 1930s.

sobbing. Elie thought he must have said something wrong about his studies. Only decades later did Elie accidentally learn, from a relative who was there that day, what news the rabbi relayed to the distraught mother. As Wiesel recounted in *All Rivers Run to the Sea*, the rabbi told his mother, "Sarah, I know your son will become a *gadol b'Yisrael* [great man in Israel], but neither you nor I will live to see the day."

CHAPTER TWO

HITLER'S CAMPAIGN AGAINST JEWS

I n 1943, as war drew closer to their village, the peaceful way of life for Jews in Sighet was in peril. The outside world was growing increasingly more dangerous for Jews. Big changes would come for Elie and his family very soon.

In his memoirs, Wiesel writes of Gentile friends in Sighet wearing masks and horns while carrying whips on Christmas Eve and taking part in a vicious hunt for Jews. Sadly, Elie came to expect anti-Jewish hatred. From the beginning, he saw that the problem belonged to the persecutors, not the victims. It was this mindset, however, that would pave the way for the Holocaust.

A MADMAN'S PLANS

In 1933, Nazi Party leader Adolf Hitler had become chancellor of Germany. The crazed dictator soon took on total power and began

Adolf Hitler took advantage of Germany's weaknesses, including a dire economy and low national morale, that came as a result of the nation's World War I defeat. With promises to rebuild the country, the madman shrewdly built up a strong sense of nationalism in Germany that fueled his goal to take over Europe.

his plan of persecuting German Jews. This began with boycotting Jewish businesses, graduated to destroying synagogues and homes, and culminated in forcing Jews to concentration camps.

Hitler also began a plan to expand Germany's borders by taking over much of Europe. In 1938, European leaders met with Hitler in Munich and gave him the Czechoslovak region of the Sudetenland. Their hope in signing the Munich Agreement was to appease the Führer so that he would be satisfied. In truth, this policy had the effect of abandoning Czechoslovakia, a democratic country that other free nations were obligated to protect.

Furthermore, the Munich Agreement marked Hitler's transition from diplomatic maneuvering to outright aggression. Soon, the first refugees from Czechoslovakia began arriving in Sighet. Elie Wiesel was ten years old. He barely noticed the Anschluss, Germany's absorption of Austria in 1938, or Hitler's invasion of Poland the following year.

The Fasanenstrasse Synagogue in Berlin was one of many Jewish places of worship set on fire by Nazi mobs during Kristallnacht in 1938. Unbelievably, officials were instructed to let them burn. Jews lost their businesses and places of worship in these orchestrated riots. Kristallnacht is considered to be the beginning of the Holocaust.

Only a boy, Elie paid little attention to the Nuremberg Laws that were enacted, stripping German Jews of all rights and discriminating against them in every walk of life. Not being interested in sports, Elie hardly followed the Olympic Games at which Hitler hoped his Aryan supermen would vanquish what he considered inferior races such as Jews, blacks, and Slavs.

Kristallnacht (Night of Broken Glass) was an organized pogrom targeting Jewish shops, homes, and houses of worship. The Wiesels read about this terrible riot that erupted throughout Germany. More than a thousand synagogues and seven thousand Jewish businesses were burned. Ninety-six Jews were killed, and Jewish cemeteries were looted along with other Jewish property such as hospitals, schools, and homes.

The danger seemed remote, however. The Wiesels still hoped the Third Reich would crumble under its own weight or be stopped by the great powers of Europe. Excessive optimism and faith in mankind prevented the Wiesels and other Jews from leaving Europe while they still could.

LIFE IN SIGHET

Originally part of Romania, Sighet was annexed—with Nazi approval—by Hungary. Perhaps the Jews of Sighet felt a false sense of security because Hungary, although allied with Germany, initially

KRISTALLNACHT

On the night of November 9, 1938, German Nazis set out to terrorize Jews throughout Germany. On direct orders from Adolf Hitler, they broke into Jewish businesses, then ransacked and looted them. They burned synagogues. They enacted violence against Jewish citizens.

The horrific event was given the name Kristallnacht, meaning "crystal night," from the broken glass that littered the streets of the Jewish quarter. One thousand synagogues and 7,500 Jewish businesses were destroyed. Nearly 100 Jews were killed in the violence, which stretched into the next day.

Kristallnacht was a direct response to an incident that involved the shooting of a German diplomat by a Jewish student. But it was really just a convenient excuse for Hitler to set in motion his horrific plan of terror. On this night, he instructed firefighters to let Jewish businesses and synagogues burn. He instructed policemen to arrest victims, not the perpetrators.

As a result, more than 30,000 Jews were arrested. Since there were not enough prisons to contain them, they were sent to concentration camps. Not long after Kristallnacht, Jews were banned from public schools, curfews were imposed on them, and they were not

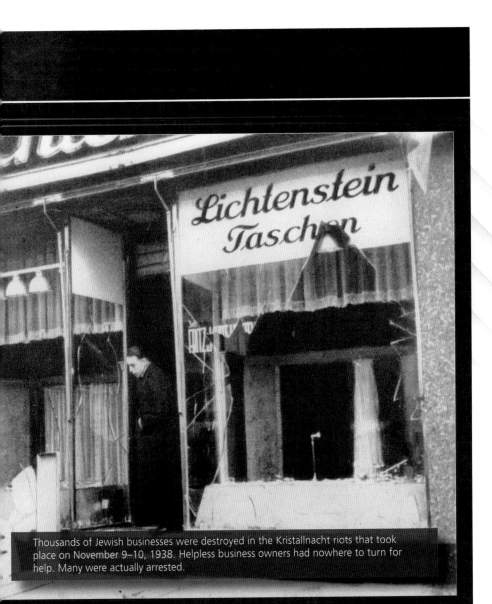

Thousands of Jewish businesses were destroyed in the Kristallnacht riots that took place on November 9–10, 1938. Helpless business owners had nowhere to turn for help. Many were actually arrested.

allowed in most public places. As we now know, things would grow much worse. For Jews in Germany, Kristallnacht marked the end of life as they knew it.

treated the Jews there as it saw fit. Except for discrimination at the university and major academies,
Hungarian Jews had less cause for complaint than
in other parts of Europe. In
Hungary, synagogues were
packed, as were Jewish
elementary and secondary
schools. Yeshivas (Jewish
religious schools of higher
education) flourished. Jewish
commerce was booming, as
were Jewish cultural centers,
sports clubs, and Zionist
organizations. Jewish semi-
nars, field trips, and debates
could be held openly and
legally.

That may explain why
the Jews in Sighet failed to
become sufficiently con-
cerned when Paris fell to the
Nazis, when Germany won
victories in North Africa,
and when the Japanese
bombed Pearl Harbor. The
Wiesel family followed these
developments by listening to
Radio London and broadcasts
from Moscow. Italian troops
passed through Sighet on
the way to the front. Jewish

refugees from Poland arrived in search of money
and false papers so the gendarmes wouldn't expel
them.

In Poland, Jews were rounded up, driven from their homes, and annexed into ghettos after Hitler invaded the country in 1939, beginning World War II. Nazi officers routinely inspected, bullied, and humiliated Jews before eventually sending them off to work camps.

The situation gradually grew worse, but the Jews of Sighet—and of many small towns and cities across Europe—couldn't imagine the horror that awaited them. Some families did leave for America, Palestine, England, South Africa, or even China while immigration was still possible. Most waited until the doors locked behind them and there was no way out.

ELIE LEARNS TO COPE

As the situation grew worse for Jews in Sighet, Elie could no longer afford to ignore what he saw and began asking why his Christian neighbors behaved so badly. Elie's teachers responded by reciting the history of Jewish persecution dating back to the biblical patriarch Abraham. "Better to be among the victims than the killers," Elie learned from the Talmud.

Elie became increasingly frightened by the rise of the Iron Guard and its anti-Semitic agenda. Slogans like "Jews to Palestine" (meaning: "Jews get out of here") began to appear on the walls of Elie's town. On days that were particularly dangerous, Elie's father told his children to stay home from *heder*. The Wiesels would bolt shut the door to their grocery store and escort regular customers through their living room and then into the back of the store.

During pogroms—periods in which Jews were killed, often with the approval of local authorities—

the family hid in the basement. Wiesel's Jewish studies helped fortify him spiritually against this onslaught. He learned about other periods in history when his people's martyrs had the courage to maintain their religious beliefs in the face of persecution.

Some Jews, a few of Elie's relatives among them, took the opportunity to escape to the Soviet Union. The Jews were imprisoned in an empire of Russian penal camps later called the Gulag.

One person from Sighet who had attempted to escape the Gulag managed to return to Sighet. He told his fellow townsfolk that Jews had been slaughtered and buried naked in ditches. But the desperate witness was considered mad; few of the Jews heeded his warning to leave Sighet.

When Elie subsequently asked his father if the family could go to Palestine, the senior Wiesel responded that he was too old to start over in a new country. Mr. Wiesel would not have offered this response had he known about Hitler's Final Solution to the so-called Jewish problem: the extermination of every Jewish person regardless of age, profession, practice, belief, or political orientation.

CHAPTER THREE

THE NAZIS ADVANCE

As Poland became unsafe for Jews, many fled for safer locations, including Hungary, which now included Romania. Shlomo Wiesel was in a position to help these refugees. By giving them foreign currency, he could ensure they would not be sent back to Poland if caught by authorities. It so happened that anyone caught with currency from another country was automatically sent to Budapest to the counterespionage bureau. Shlomo Wiesel supplied Polish Jews with American dollars and Swiss francs in hopes of saving their lives.

As the Germans advanced, nearing his home, Elie Wiesel retreated further into the world of religion, where he contemplated the nature of God. One of his teachers, Kalman the Kabalist, advised that Hitler should be resisted through piety and prayer.

During this turbulent time, Elie was having a stormy adolescence. He was still insecure, prone to outbursts of jealousy and anger if two of his peers became too close. Sometimes he stayed awake all night, feeling rejected.

However, Elie also developed strong bonds of friendship. Itzu Goldblatt and Elie competed over everything religious—even who would be the first to see the prophet Elijah in his dreams. It was Itzu who gave Elie his initial lesson in English, the language of what would one day become Elie's adopted country.

THE GERMANS COME TO SIGHET

On Sunday, March 19, 1944, Elie was in the House of Study reciting prayers. It was two days before the celebration of Purim, which commemorates the exploits of another tyrant—Haman—who sought to destroy the Jews in ancient Persia. Suddenly, a man interrupted the religious service to report that the Germans had crossed the border and were occupying the country.

Although everyone agreed that this news was terrible, few foresaw what lay ahead. Even though the Red Army was making headway against Germany, the Allied invasion at Normandy would take place soon, and Adolf Hitler's Third Reich was essentially doomed, no one warned the Jews of Sighet or tried to save yet another community slated for annihilation. Berlin needed every train for the war effort, yet railcars were

Nazi troops finally arrived in Hungary in 1944. Beginning in May of that year, Hungarian Jews were collected and transported to the Auschwitz concentration camp in Poland. The Wiesels and their fellow countrypeople had been spared for so much of the war that this must have come as a great shock.

diverted to take Jews to concentration camps. Hitler's "war against the Jews" took priority over his fight against the Allied forces.

The local fascists began preying on Jews with increased feroc-ity. They threw Jewish students from moving trains and attacked Jew-ish women. The govern-ment in Budapest issued decrees closing Jewish stores and forbidding Jews from leaving home except during certain hours. Jewish state employees were fired. Jews were no longer allowed to walk in munic-ipal parks, go to the mov-ies, or take buses, trams, and trains.

A few days before Passover, the holiday commemorating the Israelites' escape from slavery in ancient Egypt, German troops in black

THE WARSAW GHETTO UPRISING

The Warsaw Ghetto uprising took place in the spring of 1943. Between July and September of the previous year, approximately 300,000 Jews had been shipped from Warsaw, Poland, to the death camp of Treblinka. Only 50,000 Jews were left in the ghetto.

In April of 1943, these remaining Jews rose up and fought against the Nazis. The Germans had planned to liquidate the ghetto in three days, but the underground fighters held out for nearly a month. With virtually no training and a limited number of guns, rifles, and explosives, these Jewish men and women fought longer than the French army against the might of heavily armed German forces. This historic uprising took place nearly a year before Sighet was invaded.

Though ultimately unsuccessful, the Warsaw Ghetto Uprising was a heroic attempt to retaliate against the Nazis. The Warsaw Ghetto Uprising was the largest revolt by one group of Jews during the war.

uniforms arrived in Sighet. Tanks, jeeps, and motorcycles rolled through the streets. On the seventh day of Passover, which traditionally symbolized the miraculous crossing of the Red Sea, a series of new decrees were issued. The town crier, a hunchback carrying a drum that was too big for him, announced the bad news. (The synagogues had already been shut down.) All offices belonging to Jews were closed. Jews were allowed to leave home only in the late afternoon to buy food.

Shlomo Wiesel was technically no longer allowed to sell anything, but the shelves in his store were soon empty. Elie's father gave customers whatever they wanted, whether or not they paid. Elie and his sisters helped.

Three days of curfew followed. All Jews had to sew yellow Stars of David onto their clothing as a form of identification. Elie wore his proudly, feeling that this insignia connected him to the Jews of the Middle Ages and other periods of persecution.

Posters, signed by the German military governor, suddenly appeared on walls. These signs warned that anyone who opposed the new world order would be shot. Special units of the army and gendarmerie began raiding Jewish homes. Inspections and searches were conducted. Jews were threatened. All jewelry, silver, gold, precious stones, foreign currency, and objects of value belonging to Jews had to be surrendered. Anyone who resisted was beaten by the soldiers. Elie's

In accordance with Hitler's orders, Nazi officers forced Jews to identify themselves by wearing yellow Stars of David sewn onto their clothing.

father tried to joke about the situation: "The only thing they'll find in most Jewish homes is poverty. I hope they confiscate that, too." However, even poor families often had silver candlesticks or Kiddush cups (for blessing ritual wine on the Sabbath). Many Jews tried to hide these heirlooms in cellars or attics.

The Hungarians carried out Hitler's orders with great cruelty. They trampled on old people and the sick, attacked women and children. The Jews were practically relieved when the announcement came that they would be segregated into a ghetto—away from the sadists.

MISSED OPPORTUNITY

Around the time the ghetto was formed in Sighet, Maria—the Wiesels' Christian housekeeper who had worked for the family since Elie was born—offered to hide her employers at her cabin in a remote mountain hamlet. The kindhearted woman assured the Wiesels that there was room for everyone. Maria begged the Wiesels to go, insisting she would bring all the food and provisions they would need. Like the famous Frank family, the Wiesels might have hidden from the Nazis during the war. However, without information about the death camps, Shlomo Wiesel didn't realize that he needed to save his family—not just from hardship, but from murder.

The failure to see the Nazis for what they were is a psychology lesson about the power of denial. After all, Adolf Hitler spelled out the plan to exterminate the Jews in *Mein Kampf* (My Struggle), written in 1924 and published in translation in 1940. Even if the Wiesels hadn't read the book, why didn't anyone else explain it? Journalists, leaders, historians, or policy analysts could have warned the Jews.

People in other parts of the world turned a blind eye to what was happening. And some did not know what was happening until it was much too late because the Nazi propaganda machine fooled many. Most likely no one—at least not anyone with faith in humanity—could have believed just how far Hitler would be able to get with his murderous plan.

CHAPTER FOUR

DESCENT TO HELL

The Wiesels did not accept Maria's offer to move to her cabin and live in hiding, safe from the Nazis. They remained in their own home, which happened to be located within the boundaries of the designated Jewish quarter. But it wasn't quite the same as it had been. Many of the Wiesels' relatives moved into the house with them. Elie, his parents, and his sisters lived in the house's largest room, while their relatives took up residence in other parts of the modest home.

Most Jews in Sighet were forced to give up everything they had accumulated over a lifetime. There was hardly any space in the small room or cellar to which a whole family typically was assigned to keep any possessions. In addition, the Germans demanded that the ghettos supply a daily battalion of Jewish laborers. Lists were drawn up, and few people avoided the draft. Failing to comply would have put other Jews at risk, who would be selected to replace the absent workers.

Jews driven out of Czechoslovakia had arrived in Sighet, hoping for safety. However, many of these refugees were faced with the exact fate they were hoping to avoid once the SS arrived in Sighet and occupied the village.

DRIVEN FROM HOME

One Saturday in May, about a month after the ghetto had been formed, two Gestapo officers arrived at the Wiesel house. (Afterward, Elie was told that one of the men was a high-ranking Nazi official, Adolf Eichmann.) The Council of the Elders was summoned for an emergency. Transports to expel all Jews from Sighet had been planned. The first convoy was to begin the next morning, but Elie's street was not part of that group.

The Wiesels spent the night helping friends prepare to go. The rumor in the ghetto was that the Jews were being taken to a Hungarian labor camp where families would be allowed to stay together.

On May 16, the Wiesels' turn came. "All Jews out!" the soldiers screamed. The previous night, the Wiesels had dug a dozen holes under trees to hide what remained of their money and precious objects. Elie buried the gold watch he had been given as a Bar Mitzvah present. The family imagined that someday when this nightmare finally ended, everyone would be able to return to their home. Two decades later, Elie would indeed return—without his parents and little sister.

On the Tuesday afternoon in 1944 when the Wiesels were driven from their home, the train they were supposed to take wasn't ready to leave. Elie and his family were transferred for several days to the smaller ghetto whose inhabitants had already been expelled. The Wiesels moved into the home of Mendel, Shlomo Wiesel's brother, and his family.

In the house where these relatives had lived, the Wiesels found sacred books scattered across the floor. Someone must have removed the volumes from Uncle Mendel's bag at the last minute. The table was set, and food remained on the plates. The family seemed to have been taken away in the middle of a meal.

Years later, Elie learned some of what happened to Uncle Mendel. Mendel's son had stayed in his father's bunk one night at the camp. The next day an SS officer shot the boy in the head when he discovered that he was not in his assigned place. The distraught Mendel threw himself on his son's body as if to save him from death. The SS man then shot Mendel, too.

THE CONVOY

Before leaving Uncle Mendel's home, Elie's mother cooked her family's favorite food: latkes (potato pancakes). After a few days, the Wiesels were led to the train station, where they were loaded into cattle cars. Ever since, Elie Wiesel freezes each time he hears a train whistle.

Wiesel has written that life in the cattle cars spelled the end of his adolescence. The hunger, thirst, heat, and stench were all unbearable. The trains had no toilets or provisions for washing. Blankets were held up to give people a modicum of privacy while relieving themselves into a pail.

The prisoners ate whatever food they had brought with them: hard-boiled eggs, dried cakes, or fruit. Elie's mother kept repeating to her family:

"Stay together at all costs." Someone asked what to do if they were separated. "Then we'll meet again at home as soon as the war is over," Sarah Wiesel replied.

ARRIVAL AT AUSCHWITZ

Thus passed the last hours Elie spent with his family. After midnight the train pulled into a station of some type. Through the cracks in the cattle car's slats, Elie saw barbed wire stretching for what seemed like eternity. Pulled to his feet, Elie was pushed toward the door. Barked orders shattered the darkness. The family managed to stay together, as Mrs. Wiesel had instructed. Then a command was issued: "Men to the left! Women to the right!" Wiesel recalls in *Night*:

Eight words spoken quietly, indifferently, without emotion. Eight short, simple words. Yet that was the moment when I parted from my mother. I had not had time to think, but already I had felt the pressure of my father's hand: We were alone. For a part of a second I glimpsed my mother and my sisters moving away to the right. Tsiporah

This is the view the Jewish captives experienced as their cattle cars pulled in to the Auschwitz concentration camp. Elie Wiesel and his family did not know what to expect, but surely they could not have anticipated the unspeakable evil with which they would soon be faced.

held Mother's hand. I saw them disappear into the distance; my mother was stroking my sister's fair hair, as though to protect her, while I walked on with my father and the other men. And I did not know that in that place, at that moment, I was parting from my mother and Tsiporah forever.

German Nazi doctor Josef Mengele was known as the Angel of Death. Mengele carried out unethical and sadistic experiments on the concentration camp prisoners during the Holocaust.

An order was given to form lines. A Jewish inmate near Elie asked his age and that of his father. Elie replied that he was not yet fifteen, and his father was fifty. The prisoner told Elie to say that he was eighteen and his father forty. The SS guards wouldn't spare people they considered too young or old to work. Another man pointed to the chimney and flames, telling Elie that he and his family would soon be turned to ashes.

Before long, Elie and his father were standing before Josef Mengele, the cruel Nazi doctor known for performing medical research on twins. Mengele froze people alive to study how long it takes the human body to die. He also carried out other terrible experiments that killed or maimed his victims. This man carried a baton and waived for people to walk one way or the other: to the gas chambers or to barracks where survivors would be worked to death. Elie told Mengele that he was eighteen and a farmer, not a student. Mengele pointed to the left for both Elie and his father. The new inmates didn't know which way led to life. Someone told Elie and Shlomo they were heading for the crematory.

THE ANTECHAMBER OF HELL

Wiesel recalls seeing flames leaping from a ditch nearby and then a man delivering a load of babies

JOSEF MENGELE

Nicknamed the "Angel of Death," Joseph Mengele was a German physician and diehard Nazi. He was appointed chief doctor at Birkenau, the Auschwitz subcamp where Elie Wiesel first arrived.

Mengele carried out inhumane and unethical experiments on the camp's prisoners. His goal was to explore and improve fertility, in an effort to expand the German race. Mengele is best known for his research on twins. He performed experiments on many Jewish and Gypsy twins in the camp, most of whom were children. Here he was free to undertake experiments that could be cruel and even deadly.

Mengele was also responsible for selecting prisoners for execution, which is why Elie Wiesel was faced with him upon arrival. In other words, Mengele had the godlike power of deciding who would live and who would die.

Unfortunately, Josef Mengele was never made to pay for his crimes. When the war ended, he escaped from U.S. custody and lived underground, eventually fleeing to South America. There he joined other Nazis who also had managed to escape Europe. Mengele is believed to have died of a stroke in 1979.

to be burned in the ditch. Elie could not believe what he saw and thought he was having a nightmare. He decided to throw himself upon the electric wires and die quickly, but just before reaching the pit of flames, the group was told to turn left and walk toward the barracks.

This long building, with some skylights, looked to Elie "like the antechamber of Hell." Inside, the Jews were forced to strip, keeping only their belts and shoes. Guards kept beating the naked prisoners. Next the inmates were taken to the barber, who used clippers to remove all hair from their heads and bodies. Milling around, people greeted friends they recognized despite their changed appearance. Everyone was weeping.

Close to five o'clock in the morning, the kapos (prisoners who were assigned as guards) drove the group out of the barracks. Elie and his father were forced to run with the others to another barracks where all the new arrivals were soaked in disinfectant followed by a hot shower. They were made to run to a storage room full of striped, skimpy uniforms. After dressing, the men were ordered to stand for hours in the mud. Finally, an SS officer came and told the prisoners that they were in Auschwitz concentration camp. If anyone didn't work, he would be sent straight to the furnace.

Skilled workers—locksmiths, watchmakers, electricians—were separated from the rest. Elie

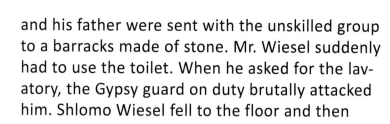

Auschwitz was a network of concentration camps. During the course of the war, more than one million prisoners died there. This photograph shows barracks at Auschwitz-Birkenau, where the Wiesel family was taken.

and his father were sent with the unskilled group to a barracks made of stone. Mr. Wiesel suddenly had to use the toilet. When he asked for the lavatory, the Gypsy guard on duty brutally attacked him. Shlomo Wiesel fell to the floor and then crawled back on all fours to his son.

They were still alive, but they were living a nightmare. Elie and his father had no idea what was in store for them. Soon they and many other prisoners were transported to the main part of Auschwitz. There they were assigned to their new home, Block 17.

CHAPTER FIVE

PRISONER A-7713

The next morning, Elie awoke to find that what they had experienced was not a nightmare but a twisted reality. He and his fellow prisoners, including his father, were rounded up and tattooed with identification numbers they had been issued by camp officials. Each person's number appeared in permanent ink on his left arm. Elie's number was A-7713.

This dehumanizing action was a way to suppress the prisoners' individuality so that it would be easier to treat them as subhuman. Having already been stripped of all signs of personal identity—property, clothing, and even their hair—the Jews now had their names taken from them.

These numbers were checked repeatedly at roll calls. Military marches were often played. Like the strange sign that hung at the entrance gate to Auschwitz—stating, in German "Work makes you free"—the music was part of a cruel hoax. In truth, work would not set Jews free; inmates were not identical, numbered things to be counted; and the civilized culture suggested by music was absent from these brutal factories of death.

Each morning, the prisoners were given black coffee. At noon, they got watery soup. In the evening, a little bread with margarine was provided. Throughout the day, Jews were subject to beatings. At nine o'clock in the evening, everyone went to sleep—two people per bunk. At night when the inmates weren't too tired, they sang Hasidic

These Hungarian Jews were selected for forced labor in the Auschwitz-Birkenau camp. Like these men, Elie Wiesel and his father were shorn of their hair, made to wear striped uniforms, and tattooed with an identification number upon arrival at the camp.

melodies. Most Jews believed the war would end soon. Shlomo Wiesel assured his son that the rest of the family had probably been sent to a labor camp. The truth was too hard to bear.

BUNA

After three weeks in Auschwitz, Elie and his father were marched with a group of prisoners to a different camp: Buna. A few other children, ten to twelve years old, were also in this convoy. At both camps, there were daily labor gangs. The most important thing was to avoid the frequent "selections." People chosen at such times were sent to their deaths.

At Buna, Elie's group of prisoners was housed in two tents. The labor Elie and his father performed involved counting bolts, bulbs, and small electrical fittings. They also loaded diesel engines onto trains.

One of the foremen spotted a gold crown on one of Elie's teeth and wanted it. Elie finally

At the camps, starving and exhausted prisoners slept in overcrowded bunks. This photograph shows Elie Wiesel and his fellow prisoners at Buchenwald. Wiesel can be seen lying in the middle row, seventh from the left.

agreed to the extraction because the angry foreman was attacking Shlomo Wiesel for his inability to march well. As long as Elie tried to keep the gold tooth, the foreman retaliated against Elie's father. The man finally had a dentist from Warsaw remove it from Elie's mouth with a rusty spoon. Another time, Elie was whipped publicly until he fainted. His father had to stand helplessly and watch his son being tortured.

Elie witnessed many executions in Buna. Men were hanged for small infractions, like trying to steal soup during an air raid. On one occasion, some kapos were thought to have stolen arms, and a young boy who acted as a servant to the condemned was also killed. As always, the prisoners were made to witness the murder. When the child was hanging with his neck in a noose, his body wasn't heavy enough to break his neck or strangle him quickly. The boy struggled between life and death for more than half an hour.

IN SEARCH OF HOPE

Wiesel wrote in *Night* and elsewhere about his difficulty retaining belief in God as a benevolent, omnipotent being. If the master of the universe is good and all-powerful, how could he permit innocent children to be slaughtered? Why didn't God intervene to save his "chosen people"? If the almighty had some part in this kingdom of darkness, then he must be in a league with Hitler as some kind of cosmic sadist. Wiesel continued to challenge God and accuse him of silence or indifference. As time passed, even fear gave way to weariness. Living from day to day, hour to hour, was a struggle in the face of starvation, cold, lack of sleep, and abuse.

Once, Shlomo Wiesel was selected for death, and Elie was sent out on work detail thinking his father was being killed that day. However, miracle of miracles, upon returning to the block that night, Elie found his father still alive. Shlomo had been able to convince the SS that he was healthy enough to perform manual labor.

People in the camps who had something to live for, some source of hope, had a better chance of survival—even though, ultimately, whether one lived or died was usually a matter of chance. Some devout Jews clung to their faith in God. Others, like Elie and his father, lived for one another.

A UNITED FRONT

Winter came, and the icy wind cut through the scantily dressed prisoners like a knife. In January, Elie's right foot began to swell from the cold, and he needed an operation to save his toes. The surgery was performed without putting Elie to sleep. He soon passed out from the pain. Recovering in the camp hospital, Elie was able to sleep on sheets again and refrain from work detail. But selections were

Prisoners at the Nazi concentration camps were forced to perform labor on minimal sleep and even less food. Those who could not keep up with the grueling work were exterminated.

more frequent in the hospital. Elie had to be careful not to stay there too long, though feasting on slightly thicker soup and extra bread was tempting.

Only days after the operation, news spread throughout the camp that the front was drawing closer. The Red Army was approaching Auschwitz. The German authorities therefore decided to evacuate the prisoners. They were to be marched overland to another camp closer to the German heartland. Hospital patients would be left behind.

Suddenly, Elie had a decision to make. Should he try to walk on his foot, which was not yet fully healed, or should he stay behind at the infirmary? If he stayed, perhaps he would be liberated by the Russian troops. However, the Germans were unlikely to leave hundreds of witnesses to testify to the atrocities committed at the camp. More likely than not, all patients would be shot and cremated. The camp itself might be mined. Elie was thinking less about the prospect of death than separation from his father. The two had managed to stay together this far. Elie wanted to remain by his father's side to help him during what promised to be a long, brutal trek.

With one shoe in his hand (because it would not fit over his swollen, bandaged foot), Elie left the hospital and ran through the deep snow in search of Shlomo Wiesel. Father and son did not know what to do, but they decided to keep together and attempt the march. "Let's hope we shan't regret it, Eliezer," Shlomo told his son. Elie later learned that

RETURN TO HELL

Elie Wiesel has returned to the place of his nightmares several times. In 2006, he visited the concentration camp in Auschwitz—now a museum—with talk show host Oprah Winfrey. Wiesel took Winfrey on a tour of the camp, remembering the horrors he experienced there. He showed Winfrey Block 17, where he and his father lived for a time, and the crematorium where his mother and sister most likely perished. As the two passed a display of the thousands of shoes collected from prisoners upon arrival to the camp, Wiesel reflected on the senselessness of the Holocaust: "How many [future] Nobel Prize winners died [here] at the age of one? Two? One of them could have discovered the remedy for cancer, for AIDS...the great poets, the great dreamers."

Wiesel returned to Buchenwald in 2009, accompanying U.S. president Barack Obama and German chancellor Angela Merkel. Speaking to the crowd, Wiesel remarked, "Memory must bring people together rather than set them apart...A great man, Camus, wrote at the end of his marvelous novel, *The Plague*: 'After all,' he said, 'after the tragedy,...there is more in the human being to celebrate than to denigrate.' Even that can be found as truth—painful as it is—in Buchenwald."

the sick prisoners who stayed behind were liberated by the invading Russians eight days after the evacuation.

Elie returned to the hospital for one last night in the camp. Through frosted panes of glass, he could see bursts of light from cannons in the distance. He couldn't sleep because his foot felt like it was burning.

A GRUELING MARCH

The next day, the prisoners wrapped themselves in blankets and layers of clothing before leaving. At the last minute, the inmates were ordered to scrub the floors and clean up so the liberating army would know "there were men living here, not pigs." When the six o'clock evening bell rang, hundreds of armed SS men—with searchlights and sheepdogs—began marching the prisoners out of Buna. The snow kept falling relentlessly. Elie and his father waited for fifty-six blocks to pass before block fifty-seven was summoned.

Elie had only two pieces of bread tucked in his pocket for the journey. The SS forced the prisoners to run. Anyone who couldn't keep up was shot. The guards screamed curses at the Jews in the frigid darkness. Elie felt as though his body and self were two separate entities. The pain in his foot was nearly unbearable. Sometimes, Elie managed to fall asleep while running.

At last, the morning star appeared in a gray sky. The commandant announced that the great wave of people had covered scores of miles since leaving the camp. The prisoners passed through a deserted village. At last, the order came to rest. Exhausted Jews sunk down in the snow. Elie joined some other inmates who fell asleep in a broken-down brick factory with a collapsed roof. Elie's father soon roused his son and helped him stand. Prisoners who had been trampled or frozen to death lay in the snow. Father and son went to another shed to rest.

The next day they kept marching in the falling snow. SS guards on motorcycles drove the prisoners forward. The convoy finally reached Gleiwitz, where everyone rested for three days. The prisoners were given no food or drink. Guards stood at the door to the barracks and prevented the inmates from leaving. The military front was following the group. Gunshots could be heard. The prisoners hoped the Nazis wouldn't have time to evacuate them.

TO BUCHENWALD

On the third day, a selection was held. Elie's father was sent to the left while Elie was directed to the right. Terrified, Elie chased after his father. An SS man ran to get Elie and bring him back. In the confusion, some people—including Shlomo Wiesel—crossed back to the side of the living. Others were shot amid the chaos. The able-bodied group was marched to a field cut by railroad tracks. They waited for the train to arrive. The men were given a little bread but were forbidden to sit. Standing there, the prisoners took out their spoons and ate the snow that had accumulated on their neighbors' backs.

A long train with cattle wagons, which had no roofs, arrived at last. The prisoners were loaded aboard and the train departed. Later on, when the train stopped, the dead were thrown out. Shlomo was mistaken for one of the corpses by a grave digger, but Elie slapped his father until Shlomo's eyes opened.

The train ride lasted for ten days. When the train stopped at some stations, German workmen threw a little bread to the starving prisoners, who fought one another for the food—to the amusement of workers and spectators. Elie watched sons fight with fathers for a morsel of bread.

A hundred prisoners got into the wagon that brought the men to Buchenwald concentration camp. Only a dozen arrived alive, including Elie and his father. Shortly after arriving at Buchenwald, Shlomo Wiesel developed a high fever. Elie felt responsible because, just before an air raid, he had been unable to convince his father to get up from the snow when he collapsed from exhaustion. Shlomo was simply running out of strength.

Elie felt ashamed because he secretly hoped to be free of the burden his father represented. Of

Prisoners stand for roll call upon arrival at the Buchenwald concentration camp. Elie Wiesel and his father were forced on a "death march" to the camp as the Allies closed in on the Nazis. Unfortunately, Shlomo Wiesel did not make it out of the camp.

course, Elie still loved his father. Much has been written about "survivor guilt"—the fact that innocent victims tend to blame themselves for surviving a catastrophe while others were not as lucky. By contrast, the people actually responsible for the tragedy—in this case, the Nazis—may feel no culpability.

Elie's father hung on for several days, weak from dysentery. The guards showed no mercy to the ill, beating Shlomo over the head when he asked for a sip of water. Elie watched over him as best as he could. On the night of January 28, 1945, he climbed into the bunk above his father. When he awoke the next morning, another man was lying in Shlomo Wiesel's place.

CHAPTER SIX

A FREE MAN

Shlomo Wiesel died when Elie was sixteen. They had worked so hard to stay together, to survive the horrors that had been inflicted on them. When Elie woke up to see another man in his father's place he could scarcely believe it. He knew his father must have died in the night and been taken to the crematorium. Racked with guilt because he couldn't save his father, the young man fell into a state of lethargy.

Elie had been transferred to a children's block with six hundred other youngsters. He spent his time in a state of idleness, dreaming about food. On April 5, the camp loudspeaker ordered all prisoners to gather at the assembly place. However, older prisoners whispered to the children that the Germans were going to shoot them. The youngsters therefore refused to report and returned to the block.

An evacuation of the camp soon began, but on April 10 twenty thousand inmates were still in Buchenwald, including several hundred children. When the sirens blew for an alert, the evacuation was postponed. No one had eaten anything—except grass and a bit of potato peel—for six days.

Prisoners at Buchenwald concentration camp rejoice and embrace one another after they are freed. Allied troops arrived at the camp, the first to be liberated, in April 1945. They were horrified at what they found.

At last, the camp resistance decided to act. Gunfire broke out, and the children stayed flat on the ground in the barracks. The battle didn't last long. The SS fled. Pretty soon, the first American tank pulled up to the gates of Buchenwald. Freedom had come to the survivors.

FREE BUT ALONE

Three days later, Elie became very ill with food poisoning. He was transferred to the hospital, where he spent two weeks hovering between life and death. When Elie was able to stand and look at himself in the mirror, he saw what looked like a corpse. Wiesel explained in *All Rivers Run to the Sea* that although the survivors felt greatly relieved to be safe at last, they "were not happy" and wondered whether they would ever feel joy again. The reign of terror had ended, but for many—like Elie—liberation came too late. He was an orphan, alone in the world, searching for relatives and a place to go.

Lists were circulated with names of people who had survived, but Elie didn't find either of his big sisters' names on these papers. Elie suspected that his mother, baby sister, and grandmother had been murdered. Most survivors were afraid to go back to their hometowns and empty houses. Often, their former residences were now occupied by neighbors who had taken all the possessions left behind. In many cases, survivors who tried to go home were killed by angry Gentiles. Initially, Belgium invited four hundred Jewish youngsters from Buchenwald to move there. However, plans changed when General Charles de Gaulle learned of the children's plight and arranged for them to come to France. Elie was among them.

REUNITED

Elie and a few other boys from Sighet went by train from Buchenwald to a boarding school in France, in care of the OSE—a children's rescue society. The youngsters were settled in a group home. Leaving Buchenwald aroused mixed feelings for orphans whose parents had been killed in the camps. Many years later, in *All Rivers Run to the Sea* Wiesel described how difficult it was "to live far from my father, my father who stayed behind, in the invisible cemetery of Buchenwald. I look up at the sky, and there is his grave. When I raise my eyes to heaven, it is his grave I see."

At a splendid castle in Ecouis, Elie attended classes and began to return to "normal life." He participated in religious services, read books, played chess, sunbathed, hiked in the forest, sang songs around the campfire, and dreamed of going to Palestine. All the children still distrusted strangers and were slow to adjust to the abundance of good

After the war, Elie Wiesel was sent to a French boarding school. This group portrait from 1945 shows Wiesel, his classmates, and the staff of Ambloy, an OSE home. Elie Wiesel stands in the third row, fourth from left.

food available.

One day, the headmaster of Elie's school told him that his sister had called from Paris. She had made plans to meet Elie the next day. Elie was shocked but hopeful. Could his sister have survived? Which sister?

The next day Elie, who spoke no French yet, traveled alone to Gare Saint-Lazare. There on the platform he found Hilda, along with an Algerian Jew named Fredo who had been deported to the concentration camp at Dachau. Hilda and Fredo were engaged to be married.

Hilda had heard that Elie was dead, but she later spotted his picture in a newspaper, *Defense de la*

France. That is how she was able to track down her brother. Elie soon learned that Bea had also survived. She had returned to Sighet looking for Elie. After a wonderful reunion with Hilda, Elie returned to Ecouis.

Many months passed before Bea learned that Elie was alive. Someone in Sighet finally told her. Hilda and Bea made arrangements to meet Elie in Antwerp, the city of diamond merchants. There, the three orphans of Sarah and Shlomo Wiesel were reunited.

By 1947, the OSE hired a private tutor—François Wahl—to give Wiesel French lessons. Elie also found good instructors of Jewish philosophy, the Talmud, and other subjects. Before long, the students were transferred to Versailles and a new home called "Our Place." This institution housed not only children from Buchenwald but girls and boys who had survived the German occupation either under false identities or by hiding with Christian families.

Elie went to Paris as often as possible to see Hilda and Fredo, who became her husband. Bea was still in a D.P. camp (that is, a camp for displaced persons) in occupied Germany. Elie wrote to her every week and visited two or three times. Bea's lungs had been damaged in the camps, and the United States consequently denied her a visa to emigrate. Like thousands of other survivors, she was considered "undesirable" in the United States but eventually was accepted in Canada.

STUDIES IN FRANCE

Elie studied at the Lycée Maimonides, often staying there from Monday to Friday. He won a prize for writing an essay about why he couldn't describe his experiences during the Holocaust. This was a hint at his future career. At this time, Elie was painfully shy. He developed crushes on a number of girls and yearned for love.

As Elie's teen years drew to a close, he enrolled at the prestigious Sorbonne, where he was quite happy. Elie devoured books. He loved attending lectures, and he took courses in philosophy and psychology, among other classes at the university. Financially, he struggled to live on a meager sum provided by the OSE. Like everyone else, he had ration cards. Elie made a little money tutoring a doctor's son in the Bible and Hebrew.

However, despite the return to a more peaceful life, Elie still became despondent and thought about committing suicide. These feelings would persist for weeks, if not months.

Newspapers fascinated Wiesel, and he always read them—regardless of the expense. Increasingly, he followed the news in Palestine and elsewhere in the world. The United Nations had voted that Jews had a right to a national homeland in Israel, and it passed the partition plan of November 29, 1947. An exuberant Wiesel rushed to the Jewish Agency in Paris and tried to join the Israeli defense force, Haganah.

Although he failed to become a soldier, another impulsive act did bear fruit. Elie wrote a patriotic letter about how he wanted to serve the Jewish resistance in Palestine. He mailed the piece to a print shop owned by a leading militant in the Zionist organization led by Vladimir Jabotinsky.

That very week Elie was invited to the newspaper's secret editorial headquarters and offered a job as a journalist. He was to receive what seemed like a millionaire's salary, thirty thousand francs a month (compared to a fraction of that amount on which he had been trying to live). Elie was able to afford a room closer to the center of town—an apartment with a sink, in fact. Bursting with energy, he moved into the Hotel de France.

CHAPTER SEVEN

FINALLY, A JEWISH STATE

Wiesel worked as a copy boy and messenger in Paris. He was there on May 14, 1948, a historic day for the Jewish people. On that day, Wiesel listened to Israeli prime minister David Ben-Gurion's reading of Israel's Declaration of Independence. At last, a Jewish state had been established.

This came after thousands of years of exile. Jews had been expelled from the land of Israel in the time of the ancient Romans and then settled in other countries that never fully accepted them. Prejudice had developed against the Jews, whose religion, culture, and history differed from the

Prime minister David Ben-Gurion reads out the proclamation of the independent state of Israel on the eve of independence, May 13, 1948.

majority. The Holocaust was one of the ugly results of intolerance. However, throughout the centuries, Jews never forgot their homeland or the Hebrew language. With the creation of Israel, Jews were able to regain control of their ancestral homeland.

At first, far away in Paris, Wiesel lived through Israel's struggle vicariously. In June, however, he earned the right to publish a story of his own about Israel. It was a fictional commentary on the tragedy of the *Altalena*—a ship filled with Holocaust survivors, munitions from France, and Jewish fighters from the Irgun and Lehi (separate pre-state armies). Presumably out of fear of a political coup, Jewish members of the Tsahal (Israel's regular army) fired on the ship when it came into Tel Aviv harbor. Many Jews were injured or killed. Wiesel was distraught that Jewish brothers should turn against one another, like the biblical Cain and Abel, Isaac and Ishmael, Jacob and

Israelis at a Tel Aviv beach watch the *Altalena* burn in June 1948. Elie Wiesel used the tragedy as a backdrop in a fictional piece he was inspired to write.

Esau, or Judah and Israel. In the piece Wiesel wrote, two brothers found themselves fighting on opposite sides when the *Altalena* was attacked.

A VISIT TO THE HOMELAND

With the help of friends, Wiesel obtained press credentials to work as a freelance writer in Israel, covering the lives of new immigrants to the Jewish state. He traveled with the settlers on a ship called the *Negba*. This first trip to Israel was bittersweet for Wiesel as he thought about the loved ones who were absent from the thrilling voyage.

He crisscrossed Israel from the Galilee to Mount Carmel, from the seashore to the desert. Because he'd been raised in the mountains, Wiesel found himself mystified by the ocean. From Haifa's window on the Mediterranean Sea to Jerusalem's view of the Judean desert, Wielsel loved Israel's varied topography. Years later, in 1967, his book *A Beggar in Jerusalem* revealed some of the author's impressions of the holy city.

Wiesel extended his stay in Israel and worked for a while as a counselor in a home for adolescents of Romanian and Bulgarian origin. As the autumn rains

Elie Wiesel finally traveled to the Promised Land in 1948. On his trip, he visited the city of Jerusalem for the first time. Although he loved Israel, Wiesel was shocked at the country's perception of Holocaust survivors as weak.

arrived, Wiesel grew depressed and withdrew into himself. In Israel, he loved the land and the people—but he also felt alienated. When interviewing the new immigrants, especially Holocaust survivors, he learned that they were treated with mixed emotions in their new country. In particular, some Israelis failed to understand how the European Jews could have allowed themselves to be slaughtered. Many in Israel found the Shoah an embarrassing topic. It seemed to perpetuate an image of Jews as weak and vulnerable. By contrast, the new Jewish state sought to project heroic stereotypes of brave settlers in a strong citizen army.

Israelis who scorned Holocaust survivors were not aware of the shameful psychological tendency to blame the victim, rather than the perpetrator, for abuse. This was just one of the mistakes that was made in criticizing European Jewry for not resisting the Nazis. In time, Israel would begin to learn how to embrace the past as part of its collective identity rather than try to repress it.

In the meantime, a lack of understanding and respect for Holocaust survivors within Israel contributed to Wiesel's melancholy. Here he was in the land of his dreams, feeling a bit useless. He began to miss Paris with its sidewalk cafés, small shops, and strolls along the Seine River. He yearned for his friends back in France as well as the intellectual climate of a country whose love of liberty, equality, and fraternity was appealing.

REPARATIONS

As a journalist, Elie Wiesel covered the first negotiations between West Germany and Israel in 1952. Germany agreed to pay reparations to Jews for stealing their property and possessions, depriving them of freedom, forcing them to work as slave labor, and murdering their relatives.

Wiesel opposed these payments for fear that they would be misunderstood and thought to lift blame from the Nazis or place an acceptable price on human life. He did not want a premature accord to be struck between Germany and the Jewish state. He realized, however, that this money helped build the state of Israel and assisted indigent Jews. In the end, the alternative—that Germany wouldn't even be held accountable economically for what it did to the Jews—was even less appealing.

FOREIGN CORRESPONDENT

An idea occurred to Wiesel. Why not become a foreign correspondent in Paris for an Israeli newspaper? He was hired to write freelance pieces for *Yediot Achronot*, Israel's smallest and poorest daily newspaper. On an overcast day in January of 1950, Wiesel returned to Paris.

Wiesel was delighted with his first article "from our Paris correspondent." It was an interview with a diplomat at the Israeli embassy in Paris. Soon Wiesel penned a piece on Beethoven for another publication. He later wrote about this period in his life in the novel *The Town Beyond the Wall*. A vociferous reader, Wiesel continued his education by immersing himself in the works of Jean Paul Sartre, Franz Kafka, William Faulkner, and Miguel de Cervantes, among other literary giants.

Wiesel learned about the visual arts, marveling at the paintings of Goya and Velazquez in the Prado in Madrid, Spain. He visited the hilltop town of Toledo, with its beautiful old synagogue that had been converted into a church after the Jews were expelled from Spain in 1492. He saw the underground tunnel where Jews could escape to the sea if priests broke into the building. El Greco, another famous Spanish painter, had lived in this former synagogue. Wiesel met with the remnants of Jewish communities wherever he traveled. He even went to Germany and spent a terrible day at Dachau concentration camp.

Back in Paris, Wiesel was asked by the Israeli paper for which he wrote to prepare a biweekly column called "Sparks from the City of Lights." For a modest monthly salary of twenty-four thousand francs, he recounted amusing anecdotes, gossip, and stories from the world of arts and letters. He attended museum and theater openings along with various receptions. He was hired to work as a translator at the World Jewish Congress in Geneva, Switzerland. At a time when Wiesel had been making the equivalent of only fifty dollars a month, he was suddenly offered two hundred dollars a day. With four months' salary being paid for just a day's work, plus expenses, he thought he was a millionaire.

During these years, violent migraine headaches continued to plague Wiesel. These headaches can be brought on by stress. With all that he had endured in his life, it was no wonder that he was suffering. Wiesel possessed many unspoken and unresolved memories from his life in the concentration camps that would continue to haunt him for years. Would he ever live a peaceful life?

CHAPTER EIGHT

TEACHING THE WORLD

For ten years, Wiesel honored a self-imposed vow of silence, writing nothing about his experience in the concentration camps during the war. He traveled the world, studying suffering in the Hindu tradition in India and visiting Bea in Montreal. Finally, on a voyage to Brazil, he began writing an account of his time in the camps.

This was the work that became a forerunner to Wiesel's first memoir, *Night*. When he submitted his manuscript to a publisher, Wiesel was told that no one was interested in the death camps anymore and that his book wouldn't sell. However, Editions de Minuit agreed to publish the book in French under the title *La Nuit*.

This slim, heartbreaking volume did more to bring the Holocaust to world consciousness than nearly any other work ever written. "To write is to plumb the unfathomable depths of being," Wiesel explains. *Night* came out in the United States in 1960. Worldwide, the reviews were quite favorable. The book would become the first work in a trilogy that included *Dawn* and *Day*.

It was ten years before Elie Wiesel could write about his experience at Auschwitz and Buchenwald. The results were astonishing, and Wiesel's accounts of the Holocaust opened the eyes of many around the world.

IN AMERICA

After some time in Israel, Wiesel traveled to the United States. In America, Wiesel continued writing and meeting world leaders. In 1956, he met David Ben-Gurion when he was assigned to cover the Israeli prime minister's visit with President Dwight Eisenhower.

One day in July 1956 Wiesel was struck by a taxi. The entire left side of his body had been shattered. He was put in a cast from neck to foot. Wiesel could not avoid confronting the irony of having survived the death camps only to be run down on the streets of New York. His later novel *The Accident* drew upon some of his experiences recuperating. However, in this book the accident was painted as a veiled suicide attempt. Demons from the past continued to haunt Wiesel.

In following years, Wiesel became an American citizen and wrote for the *Jewish Daily Forward*, for which he covered the Adolf Eichmann trial in Jerusalem. In the mid-1960s, Wiesel met a young mother of Austrian descent who was in the process of getting a divorce. Marion had grown up in Vienna and had fled the Nazis to Belgium, France, and Switzerland with her family. At an Italian restaurant across the street from the United Nations, where he often went to cover U.N. stories, Wiesel began falling in

Wiesel met Marion, a young divorcée and mother, while working as a journalist in New York City. Marion had experienced a different childhood in Europe. Her family fled the Nazis, eventually residing in Switzerland. With Marion, Wiesel closed one chapter and opened another.

love with the beautiful woman, who later became his translator and his wife.

On April 2, 1969, in the Old City of Jerusalem, an ancient synagogue—which had been destroyed by Jordan in 1948—was opened for a wedding. Elie and Marion married on the day before Passover. At forty years of age, the groom looked back on his childhood and adolescence. How was it possible he would marry without his parents at his side? At times of transition in the life cycle, people often return to their roots and review the forces that have shaped them. Despite the love Elie felt for Marion, he was overcome by emotion in the face of so much loss.

When writing *All Rivers Run to the Sea*, Wiesel ended the volume with his marriage. In a sense, this act marked the completion of the past and a new beginning for Wiesel—he was a full adult at last. The title of the second half of his autobiography, titled *And the Sea Is Never Full*, quotes the second half of the mournful passage in Ecclesiastes: "All rivers run to the sea, and the sea is never full." The names of the two books, like the life they chronicle, form a whole.

On June 6, 1972, Marion Wiesel gave birth to a son, Shlomo Elisha Wiesel. The boy was named after Elie's father. The man who hadn't wanted to bring children into the world was now a father himself. Wiesel said that his son's birth was "a dawn unlike any other." It allowed him to choose to commit to life.

ARMENIAN GENOCIDE

During World War I (1914–1918), a mass killing of Armenians occurred in the Ottoman Empire. Concerned that the Armenians would collaborate with Russia, Ottoman authorities deported all Armenian men of military age to the desert. During this exile, hundreds of thousands of Armenians died of starvation or were killed by soldiers. Actual statistics are in dispute, but the death toll for the Armenian genocide is believed to range from 600,000 to 1,500,000.

There is much debate about whether these killings should be classified as genocide. The Turkish government contends that there was no formal policy to exterminate Armenians, while the Armenian government believes that the campaign was a deliberate attempt to destroy its people.

Elie Wiesel believes that the atrocity was indeed genocide. Although he understands the political ramifications of accusing Turkey, an ally to Israel, he has taken a stand by signing a joint declaration of Holocaust survivors who believe the Armenian genocide should be recognized by Western governments. As someone who insists that we should never forget the atrocity of the Holocaust, Wiesel likewise fights for the importance of remembering the terror of the Armenian genocide.

FINDING HIS PLACE

Wiesel's works raise painful questions that some people would prefer to forget. Wiesel soon became an educator to convey important but different lessons. Rabbi Yitz Greenberg of the Jewish studies department at City College in New York offered Wiesel a teaching post and the opportunity to give courses in Hasidic texts, Holocaust literature, Jewish studies,

Wiesel joined the faculty of Boston Universtiy and has returned many times over the years as a guest. Once he had put out his story to the world, he felt obligated to continue sharing it. Thus began Wiesel's life as an educator.

and the Talmud. Before long, President John Silber of Boston University made Wiesel the Andrew W. Mellon Professor in Humanities.

Wiesel was growing from a struggling artist into a symbol of conscience on the world stage. He began speaking out for human rights, wherever people suffer, as well as for the Jewish people. In 1975, he traveled to South Africa to oppose apartheid. In 1980, he visited Cambodia as part of a delegation to protest atrocities committed by Pol Pot and his Communist Khmer Rouge. Wiesel went to Nicaragua to meet Miskito Indians expelled from their homes by Daniel Ortega's left-wing regime. In 1985, in Arizona, Wiesel participated in the first conference to explore possibilities of political asylum for refugees from El Salvador and Guatemala. Wiesel protested terrorism in all forms: against Israelis, through plane hijackings, and the massacre of defenseless school children in Maalot; and in Northern Ireland, Sri Lanka, Lebanon, and India. Wherever people were unfairly persecuted, there was Elie Wiesel to support them.

CHAPTER NINE

BUILDING A LEGACY

Over the years, Wiesel delivered lectures around the globe. He became one of the most gifted, thought-provoking speakers in the Jewish community, if not the entire world. Wiesel had mixed feelings about his success as a speaker, writing at one point that he even came to loathe the sound of his own voice. In fact, his mellifluous voice contributed to the passionate sadness of his message.

In his speeches and writing, Wiesel approaches aspects of the Holocaust as though they are a sacred mystery. He stresses questions, rather than answers, in connection with why this tragedy occurred.

IMPORTANCE OF THE HOLOCAUST NARRATIVE

In January of 1979, Wiesel visited the White House at Jimmy Carter's request to begin work as chairman of the President's Commission on the Holocaust. From the beginning, Wiesel had doubts about his role leading an institution that would build a museum commemorating the Holocaust. Wiesel did not like fund-raising, and he distrusted museums as educational tools, preferring books for that purpose.

Despite these reservations, Wiesel lent the prestige of his name to a project that soon promised to erect a major building near the Mall in Washington, D.C. A national day of remembrance for Holocaust victims was also established.

On a fact-finding mission for the Holocaust Council, Wiesel led a painful pilgrimage back to Auschwitz. Travel to the Soviet Union on behalf of the museum allowed Wiesel to continue working for Russian Jews. Over the years, the successor body to the President's Commission, the United States Holocaust Memorial Council, hosted a number

On November 1, 1978, President Jimmy Carter established a Holocaust commission. On hand at the president's announcement were Israeli prime minster Menachem Begin and First Lady Rosalynn Carter.

of international gatherings, such as a Liberators' Conference held in October of 1981 at the State Department.

Often, Wiesel's ideals come into conflict with the world. In early 1985, President Ronald Reagan was scheduled to travel to West Germany. At the urging of Chancellor Helmut Kohl, Reagan agreed to visit a military cemetery at Bitburg where SS officers are buried. Wiesel tried to convince the president that honoring Nazi murderers was a bad idea. When Wiesel's efforts behind the scenes proved futile, the writer spoke out against the trip on national television. Wiesel had been awarded both a Presidential Medal of Freedom and a Congressional Gold Medal. Visiting Reagan at the White House, Wiesel told the president that his "place was with the victims, not the killers." Reagan's visit to Bitburg was one factor that contributed to Wiesel's resignation from the Holocaust Council.

Wiesel was also greatly disturbed by the trivialization of the Holocaust in the media. Following years in which the subject had been largely ignored, a number of television docudramas, movies, and popular discussions treated the Holocaust in ways Wiesel considered artistically unworthy or historically inaccurate. He said that only victims who were in the camps could understand what happened, while arguing simultaneously for more education about the Holocaust.

NOBEL PRIZE

In 1986, Elie Wiesel became the recipient of perhaps the greatest honor in the world. He won a Nobel Peace Prize, which he received in Oslo, Norway. He learned that he had been chosen for this award on the afternoon of Yom Kippur, the Jewish Day of Atonement. Marion and Elie started a Foundation for Humanity with the money that was part of the

Elie Wiesel was awarded a Nobel Peace Prize in 1986. His son, Elisha (*left*), was among those to attend the ceremony in Oslo, Norway. The Nobel Committee praised Wiesel for seeing "the struggle against indifference as a struggle for peace."

Nobel Prize. This institution sponsors conferences on many issues. Some colloquia were devoted to "The Anatomy of Hate"—its causes and cures.

At Boston University, participants studied religious dimensions of hatred and fanaticism. At Haifa University in Israel, the learning of hate was discussed. An international conference of Nobel laureates, which addressed the threats and promises of the twenty-first century, was held in Paris in 1988 on the anniversary of the evacuation of Auschwitz.

FIGHTING HATRED AROUND THE WORLD

The Wiesels continued to travel extensively. In the spring of 1987, Wiesel testified at the trial of Klaus Barbie—a war criminal who murdered Jews in Lyon, France. In August 1988, the Wiesels visited the Jewish community in Australia. In October of 1990, Wiesel visited Russia. The next year he was invited to Romania to commemorate the fiftieth anniversary of the pogrom that took place in June of 1941.

In the spring of 1992, in response to race riots in Brooklyn's Crown Heights neighborhood, New York governor Mario Cuomo asked Wiesel to sponsor a conference on ethnic hatred. A seminar titled "To Save Our Children" was held in the fall. Marion Wiesel worked tirelessly with the governor's staff to plan the event.

In 2006, Wiesel teamed up with broadcasting powerhouse Oprah Winfrey to educate a mass audience on the subject of the Holocaust. The pair traveled to Poland, where Wiesel led Winfrey and her cameras on a tour of the Auschwitz camp where he had

In June of 1995, an international conference devoted to "The Leaders of Tomorrow" took place in Venice, Italy. In attendance were thirty adolescents from areas of the world in conflict—the Middle East, Ireland, Yugoslavia, various African countries, and the United States.

In December, a conference on "The Future of Hope" was held at Hiroshima, Japan. Ten Nobel laureates, a former Japanese prime minister, Secretary of State Lawrence Eagleburger, nuclear experts, journalists, and economists all participated.

Wiesel went to Belgrade after being asked in July of 1992 to lead a delegation that would investigate prison camps for Bosnians in Serbia. He met with inmates in an attempt to improve conditions and prevent atrocities. Seeing how the citizens of Yugoslavia lived in their besieged cities was nearly unbearable. Sarajevo was once an example of urban coexistence. Wiesel asked what had gone wrong. He spoke out worldwide against Slobodan Milosevic's racist policy of "ethnic cleansing" and supported intervention by NATO (North Atlantic Treaty Organization).

LATER YEARS

The extraordinary course of Elie Wiesel's life has taken him far from his humble beginnings. Nevertheless, in one sense the writer's heart is still back

HOLOCAUST DENIAL

In 2007, Elie Wiesel was attacked on a hotel elevator in San Francisco by a Holocaust denier. The man demanded that Wiesel admit that the Holocaust is a myth. Fortunately, Wiesel was unhurt and the man was arrested.

Who could possibly deny that the Holocaust occurred? Incredible though it may seem, since there is so much documentation and many first-person accounts to prove it, there are people who believe the Holocaust is a myth perpetrated by Jews. These anti-Semites spread their theories and their hatred over the Internet. It is people like this who make Wiesel's message that we should learn from the horrors of the Holocaust absolutely essential.

in his hometown within a Jewish community that no longer exists there. Over Wiesel's desk in New York hangs a single photograph of his home on Serpent Street in Sighet. "When I look up, that is what I see," Wiesel explains. "And it seems to be telling me, 'Do not forget where you came from.'"

Over the years, Wiesel continued to bear witness to the evil forces that destroyed his loved ones and almost all of European Jewry. From all sides, people tried to discourage Wiesel from focusing on the past. A future-oriented America insisted that what no longer exists should be forgotten. True to his heritage and its emphasis on memory, Wiesel remained devoted to a rich tradition. Neither could he fail to recall the terrors he experienced in this most violent of centuries.

Wiesel continued to speak on the behalf of others around the world. In 2004, he urged the United Nations to intervene in Darfur, where ethnic cleansing had killed hundreds of thousands. He led a commission for a report on the history of the Holocaust in Romania, with the goal of representing Romanian Jews.

In 2002, he inaugurated the Elie Wiesel Memorial House in his hometown of Sighet. In 2006, he received knighthood from England's Queen Elizabeth. And he continues to write, receiving the Dayton Literary Peace Prize Lifetime Achievement Award.

Elie Wiesel may have already achieved as much recovery as is possible in a lifetime. The man who described himself as an unlikely survivor still can't make sense of his life. As he told Oprah Winfrey, "I can't understand it. I was the wrong person for it. I was always timid, frightened, bashful … I had never taken any initiative to try to live. I never pushed myself, never volunteered. I was the wrong person. I was always sick when I was a child."

But he did survive, and he not only managed to live a so-called normal life, but a meaningful life as well. The Holocaust will never disappear from

Wiesel visited the Buchenwald concentration camp with U.S. president Barack Obama in June 2009. Obama remarked, "More than half a century later, our grief and our outrage over what happened have not diminished."

his consciousness; and because of Wiesel's efforts, neither will it disappear from the conscience of the world. As he remarked on his return to Auschwitz, "The death of one child makes no sense. The death of millions—what sense could it make? Except for here, now we *know*. Whenever people could try to conduct such experiments against another people, we must be there to shout and say, 'No, we remember.'" As the Talmud teaches, "It is not incumbent upon you to complete a task, but neither are you exempt from beginning."

1928 Elie Wiesel is born in Sighet, Romania, on September 30.

1933 Hitler is appointed chancellor (prime minister) of the German nation. The first concentration camp opens at Dachau in March. The first laws restricting Jewish rights are passed in April.

1935 The Nuremberg Laws are passed, forbidding mixed marriages between Jews and Christians. Jews lose their rights of citizenship.

1937 The Buchenwald concentration camp opens.

1938 Kristallnacht (the Night of Broken Glass) occurs. German mobs destroy Jewish shops and synagogues.

1939 Germany invades Poland in September, beginning World War II. The Auschwitz concentration camp opens.

1940 German Jews ordered to wear yellow stars. Mass deportation of Jews to concentration camps begins. Sighet is annexed by Hungary.

1941 German Jews sent to ghetto in Lodz, Poland.

1942 Wansee Conference is held in January, in which the Final Solution, extermination, is planned for the Jews. The Treblinka death camp is opened.

1944 Sighet is occupied by Nazi forces. The Wiesel family is deported to Auschwitz. Allied forces invade Normandy, France.

1945 Shlomo and Elie Wiesel are led on a death march to Buchenwald in January. Shlomo dies. Russians capture Auschwitz in February. American troops capture Buchenwald and Bergen-Belsen concentration camps in April; Elie is liberated. Germany surrenders in May.

1948 Begins studies at the Sorbonne in France.

1949 Visits Israel for the first time.

1955 Emigrates to the United States.

1960 *Night* is released in the United States.

1969 Marries Marion Erster Rose.

1972 Marion gives birth to Shlomo Elisha.

1978–1986 Serves as chairman of the Presidential Commission on the Holocaust.

1984 Awarded U.S. Congressional Gold Medal and French Legion of Honor.

1986 Awarded Nobel Peace Prize.

1993 U.S. Holocaust Museum dedicated in Washington, D.C.

2006 Returns to Auschwitz concentration camp with Oprah Winfrey for a televised tour. Awarded honorary British knighthood.

2007 Awarded Dayton Literary Peace Prize's Lifetime Achievement.

2009 Accompanies Angela Merkel and Barack Obama on tour of Buchenwald camp.

2015 Commemoration of the seventieth anniversary of the liberation of Auschwitz.

GLOSSARY

Anschluss The union of Nazi Germany and Austria in 1938 as part of the Axis alliance.

anti-Semitism Hatred of Jews.

apartheid Policy of segregation and discrimination on the basis of race.

Aryan In Nazi ideology, a white European Gentile of Nordic type (preferably blond and light).

bar mitzvah Initiation ceremony of a Jewish boy at age thirteen.

diaspora The dispersion of Jews outside Israel and throughout the world; can also apply to other peoples dispersed outside their homeland.

Führer Leader; the title used by Adolf Hitler as head of Nazi Germany; a tyrant.

gendarmerie Military police with responsibility for public security within national territory.

genocide The systematic killing of an entire ethnic, racial, or cultural group.

Gestapo Nazi secret state police started by Hermann Göring in 1933 to terrorize people.

Gulag A vast system of prisons in the north of the Soviet Union where political prisoners were jailed.

heder School for Jewish children where they learn the Hebrew language and religious information.

Holocaust The extermination of six million Jews by Nazi Germany during World War II.

kapo Concentration camp prisoner tasked with the job of supervising fellow prisoners.

martyr Someone killed for his or her beliefs.

Nazi Party The National Socialist German Workers' Party brought to power in 1933 by Adolf Hitler.

pogrom A massacre of Jews or other minorities, often sanctioned by local authorities.

Shabbat Sabbath, on Saturday, when Jews don't work and they celebrate God's seventh day of rest.

Shoah Word used in Hebrew for the Holocaust.

SS Nazi Germany's military force.

Talmud A collection of ancient Rabbinic writings that form a basis for Jewish law.

Third Reich The rule of Adolf Hitler and the Nazis in Germany from 1933 through 1945.

Torah The Five Books of Moses, or Hebrew Bible, written by hand on a scroll of parchment.

yeshiva A religious school for Jewish students, often on the high school level.

American Society for Yad Vashem
500 Fifth Ave, 42nd Floor
New York, NY 10110
(212) 220-4304
Website: http://www.yadvashemusa.org
Yad Vashem's archives document the history of the
    Jewish people during the Holocaust period.

Association of Holocaust Organizations
P.O. Box 230317
Hollis, NY 11423
(516) 582-4571
Website: http://www.ahoinfo.org
The Association of Holocaust Organizations (AHO)
    is an international network of organizations and
    individuals for the advancement of Holocaust
    education, remembrance, and research.

Freeman Family Foundation
Holocaust Education Centre of the Jewish Heritage
    Centre of Western Canada
C140-123 Doncaster Street
Winnipeg, Manitoba R3N 2B2
Canada
(204) 477-7458
Website: http://www.ffhec.org
The mandate of the Holocaust Education Centre is

to raise awareness and understanding of the history of the Shoah through education. Visitors can view artifacts from Holocaust survivors as well as special exhibits.

The Montreal Holocaust Memorial Centre
5151 Cote Ste. Catherine Road
Montreal, Quebec H3W 1M6
Canada
(514) 345-2605
Website: http://www.mhmc.ca/en
The Montreal Holocaust Memorial Centre educates
    people of all ages and backgrounds about the
    Holocaust, while sensitizing the public to the uni-
    versal perils of antisemitism, racism, hate, and
    indifference. Through its museum, its commem-
    orative programs and educational initiatives, the
    center promotes respect for diversity and the
    sanctity of human life.

Museum of Jewish Heritage: A Living Memorial to
    the Holocaust
36 Battery Place
New York, NY 10280
(646) 437-4202
Web site: http://www.mjhnyc.org
The Museum of Jewish Heritage offers exhibits
    chronicling the Jewish experience in the twenti-
    eth and twenty-first centuries. Using first-person
    narratives and personal artifacts, it includes a
    collection of memories of Holocaust survivors.

Museum of Tolerance New York
226 East 42nd Street
New York, NY 10017
(212) 697-1180
Website: http://www.museumoftolerancenewyork.
com
Through interactive workshops, exhibits, and videos,
visitors can explore issues of prejudice, diversity,
tolerance, and cooperation in the workplace, in
schools, and in the community.

Simon Wiesenthal Center and Museum of Tolerance
1399 South Roxbury
Los Angeles, CA 90035
(800) 900-9036
Website: http://www.wiesenthal.com
The Simon Wiesenthal Center is a global human
rights organization researching the Holocaust
and hate in a historic and contemporary context.

United States Holocaust Memorial Museum
100 Raoul Wallenberg Place
Washington, DC 20024
(202) 488-0400
Website: http://www.ushmm.org
With powerful exhibits containing artifacts from
the Holocaust and special programs, the United
States Holocaust Memorial Museum inspires
citizens and leaders worldwide to confront
hatred, prevent genocide, and promote human
dignity.

USC Shoah Foundation
650 W. 35th Street, Suite 114
Los Angeles, CA 90089
(213) 740-6001
Website: https://sfi.usc.edu
The Shoah Foundation is dedicated to recording and
    archiving video testimonies of Holocaust survi-
    vors and witnesses.

WEBSITES

Because of the changing nature of Internet links,
Rosen Publishing has developed an online list of
websites related to the subject of this book. This site
is updated regularly. Please use this link to access
this list:

http://www.rosenlinks.com/HOLO/Wiesel

Altman, Linda Jacobs. *Hitler, Goebbels, Himmler: The Nazi Holocaust Masterminds*. Berkeley Heights, NJ: Enslow Publishers, Inc., 2014.

Brezina, Corona. *Nazi Architects of the Holocaust*. New York, NY: The Rosen Publishing Group, Inc., 2015.

Byers, Ann. *Auschwitz, Bergen-Belsen, Treblinka: The Holocaust Camps*. Berkeley Heights, NJ: Enslow Publishers, 2014.

Byers, Ann. *Saving Children from the Holocaust: The Kindertransport*. Berkeley Heights, NJ: Enslow Publishers, 2012.

Dakers, Diane. *Elie Wiesel: Holocaust Survivor and Messenger for Humanity*. New York, NY: Crabtree Publishing Company, 2012.

Darman, Peter. *The Holocaust and Life Under Nazi Occupation*. New York: Rosen Publishing, 2013.

Deem, James M. *Auschwitz: Voices from the Death Camp*. Berkeley Heights, NJ: Enslow Publishers, 2012.

Deem, James M. *Kristallnacht: The Nazi Terror That Began the Holocaust*. Berkeley Heights, NJ: Enslow Publishers, 2012.

Fishkin, Rebecca Love. *Heroes of the Holocaust*. Mankato, MN: Compass Point Books, 2011.

Fitzgerald, Stephanie. *Children of the Holocaust*. Mankato, MN: Compass Point Books, 2011.

Fremon, David K. *Schindler, Wallenberg, Miep Gies: The Holocaust Heroes*. Berkeley Heights, NJ: Enslow Publishers, Inc., 2014.

George, Charles, and Linda George. *The Holocaust*. San Diego, CA: ReferencePoint Press, 2012.

Haugen, David M. *The Holocaust*. Farmington Hills, MI: Greenhaven Press, 2011.

Machajewski, Sarah. *Elie Wiesel: Speaking Out Against Genocide*. New York, NY: Rosen Publishing, 2015.

Peppas, Lynn. *The Holocaust*. New York, NY: Crabtree Publishing Company, 2015.

Perl, Lila. *The Holocaust*. New York, NY: Marshall Cavendish Benchmark, 2012.

Rappaport, Doreen. *Beyond Courage: The Untold Story of Jewish Resistance During the Holocaust*. Somerville, MA: Candlewick Press, 2012.

Sheehan, Sean. *Why Did the Holocaust Happen?* New York, NY: Gareth Stevens, 2011.

Stille, Darlene R. *Architects of the Holocaust*. Mankato, MN: Compass Point Books, 2011.

Thomson, Ruth. *Terezín: Voices from the Holocaust*. Somerville, MA: Candlewick Press, 2011.

Wiesel, Elie. *All Rivers Run to the Sea: Memoirs*. New York: Knopf , 1995.

Wiesel, Elie. *The Night Trilogy*. New York, NY: Hill and Wang, 1985.

Yeatts, Tabatha. *Wiesel, Wiesenthal, Klarsfeld: The Holocaust Survivors*. Berkeley Heights NJ: Enslow Publishers, 2014.

INDEX

ABOUT THE AUTHORS

Jean Silverman has studied and taught European history, particularly the history of the Holocaust.

Linda Bayer earned a PhD in education and psychology from Harvard University. Bayer was an award-winning reviewer at the *Washington Jewish Week*.

PHOTO CREDITS

Cover Ulf Andersen/Hulton Archive/Getty Images; p. 5 Ryan Donnell/Aurora// Getty Images; pp. 6-7 (background) Ingo JezierskiPhotographer's Choice/Getty Images; pp. 6-7 (inset) © ZUMA Press, Inc./Alamy; pp. 10, 15, 26, 36, 48, 62, 71, 80, 88 Rolf E. Staerk/ Shutterstock.com;pp. 12-13 United States Holocaust Memorial Museum, courtesy of Mitchell Eisen; pp. 16-17 Roger Viollet/ Getty Images; p. 18 Hulton Archive/Getty Images; pp. 20-21, 40-41, 54, 71 (inset) ullstein bild/Getty Images; pp. 22-23 Sovfoto/Universal Images Group/ Getty Images; pp. 28-29, 49 Galerie Bilderwelt/Hulton Archive/Getty Images; pp. 30-31 Universal History Archive/UIG/Getty Images; pp. 33, 46-47 © SZ Photo/Scherl/The Image Works; p. 37 Popperfoto/Getty Images; p. 42 Hulton Archive/Archive Photos/Getty Images; pp. 50-51 H. Miller/Hulton Archive/ Getty Images; pp. 60-61 United States Holocaust Memorial Museum, American Jewish Joint Distribution Committee, courtesy of Robert A. Schmuhi; p. 63 Margaret Bourke-White/The LIFE Picture Collection/Getty Images; pp. 66-67 United States Holocaust Memorial Museum, courtesy of Jacques Ribons; pp. 72-73 AFP/Getty Images; pp. 74-75 Frank Scherschel/The LIFE Picture Collection/Getty Images; p. 81 Keystone-France/Gamma-Keystone/Getty Images; pp. 82-83 Yvonne Hemsey/Hulton Archive/Getty Images; p. 86 The Boston Globe/ Getty Images; p. 89 Jimmy Carter Library; p. 91 Inge Gjellesvik/AFP/Getty Images; p. 93 Jemal Countess/WireImage/Getty Images; p. 97 © dpa picture alliance archive/Alamy; interior pages background textures and graphics Aleksandr Bryliaev/Shutterstock.com, kak2s/Shutterstock.com, argus/Shutterstock. com, Sfio Cracho/Shutterstock.com; back cover Ventura/Shutterstock.com.

Designer: Michael Moy; Editor: Christine Poolos; Photo Researcher: Rona Tuccillo